An Outdoor Adventure Book

WILDLIFE REFUGE

A Classroom Adventure

Lorraine Ward
Laura Jacques

🚣 Charlesbridge

ENDANGERED
PEREGRINE
FALCON

639.95
WARD, L

With appreciation for the wonderful people at Aransas National Wildlife Refuge in Texas.

With thanks to: Verplanck School, Manchester, CT

*Principal: Mr. Doug Townsend and
the 1992 3rd Grade Class of Miss O'Reilly*

Sharon Bailey, Jennifer Barbieri, Dane Bundy, Justin Clark, Nicole Everett, Grace Han, Gordon Hood, Thomas Irwin, Nathan Jackson, Gerald Jenkins, Ryan Kaiser, Charissa Kearney, Mona Khan, Paul Molinari, Marco Morelli, Kasey Quaglia, Michelle Rodriguez, Joannah Smith, Mimi Torres, Justin Turner, Tyno Vilayvong, Amanda Young

Published by
Charlesbridge Publishing
85 Main Street
Watertown, MA 02172
(617) 926-0329
www.charlesbridge.com

Printed in the United States of America
(hc) 10 9 8 7 6 5 4 3 2 1
(sc) 10 9 8 7 6 5 4 3 2 1

This book was printed on recycled paper.

Library of Congress Cataloging-in-Publication Data
Ward, Lorraine.
  Wildlife refuge: a classroom adventure / by Lorraine
Ward; illustrated by Laura Jacques.
        p.   cm.
  Summary: A class learns the purpose of a wildlife
refuge and what happens to the animals that live within
its boundaries.
  ISBN 0-88106-967-1 (reinforced for library use)
  ISBN 0-88106-964-7 (softcover)
  1. Wildlife refuges—Juvenile literature. 2. Wildlife
conservation—Juvenile literature. [1. Wildlife refuges.
2. Wildlife conservation.] I. Jacques, Laura, ill. II. Title.
QL83.W38 1993
639.9'5—dc20   93-3090
                                                          CIP
                                                          AC

Cassie and Danny were looking at a library book about a wildlife refuge. "Mr. Wilson, when are we going?" asked Cassie.

"We will be leaving soon," answered Mr. Wilson. "Remember, the animals we will be seeing today are wild. A refuge is very different from a zoo because it is there for a different reason."

The first thing they saw when they arrived at the wildlife refuge was a big map. Patti, their guide, pointed out the different parts of the refuge. "The shoreline areas are wetlands. Inland it is drier so there are different kinds of plants and animals. These lines show where the trails and picnic areas are. Let's go!"

"Why are these wooden paths here?" asked Jimmy.

Patti explained, "Most of the plants that grow here are food or homes for the animals. The wooden paths keep us from stepping on any of them."

"Why is this place a refuge?" Sara wanted to know.

"That's a good question," said Mr. Wilson. "Many of the animals that live here are rare or endangered. That means that there aren't very many of them left. Without our help, some of them may disappear soon."

"This refuge gives the animals a place to live and lets people see them and learn how to help them. Many of the animals are helped most by being left alone. Others come to raise their babies in a protected place."

The children watched a duck family swimming around. Suddenly, the ducks tipped up, burying their heads in the water.

"What are they doing?" Danny asked, laughing.

"It's called dabbling," Patti said. "They're looking for food under the water. Ducks eat water plants, insects, and tadpoles."

"Are all the animals that live here endangered?" asked Molly, who didn't think ducks seemed very rare.

"No," said Patti. "This refuge protects a few endangered species, and gives many other animals a safe place to live so that they don't become endangered."

"Where are they all?" asked Molly. "I've only seen ducks!"

"Oh, they are here," said Patti, "but you have to look carefully to see animals in the wild. For example, has anyone noticed the alligator over there?"

"Wow!" said Cassie. "I thought that was a log. Why aren't those birds afraid to walk so close to it?"

"They know that this alligator prefers to eat turtles, frogs, and fish," said Patti.

"Oh, the poor frogs," said Sara. "I thought the refuge was supposed to protect them."

Patti explained, "We protect animals by giving them the right kind of place to live where they can find their own food. That's how we are different from a zoo."

"Don't feel bad for the frogs. Without small animals, the large ones, like that white ibis, would not have any food. Without large animals, there would be too many small animals to live in this area. It's all part of what we call the balance of nature."

"There sure are a lot of birds here," Miles said as they walked onto a pier.

"Yes," said Patti, "wetlands are perfect for birds because there are crabs, snails, frogs, insects, seeds and fish that birds like to eat. Hopefully, we'll see our most famous bird, the whooping crane, from the boat."

"Fifty years ago, there were only a few whoopers left! Thanks to new laws that protect them, and to refuges like this one, there are over a hundred whoopers now," said Patti.

"Why are they called whoopers?" asked Cassie.

Patti explained, "Instead of tweeting, quacking, or chirping like other birds, they make a sound like a whoop."

"There they are," she called, pointing toward the shore.

"They're so big!" Sara said.

"Whooping cranes are America's tallest bird," Patti said. "They fly south in the fall and stay here until spring. Soon they will fly thousands of miles north to their summer nesting place."

All of a sudden, Sara spun around. "I thought I saw a dolphin," she yelled. "Over there!"
"You probably did," Patti said, as they all turned to look. A few minutes later they all saw dolphins leap out of the water.
"Look! They're coming with us," Bobby shouted.

"Here's another endangered bird," Patti called to them. "See those brown pelicans?"
The children laughed as a brown pelican dove deep into the water and came up with a
pouch full of fish.

"Wow, I wish I could catch fish that fast," said Miles.

"We can't catch fish for lunch like a pelican, but *we* have a picnic waiting for us," Mr. Wilson said as they got off the boat. While they ate, Patti told them about some of the animals to look for after lunch.

"Will we see any big cats?" asked Anita.

"Probably not," answered Patti. "The big cats that live here are the jaguarundi, the cougar and the bobcat. They hide by day and hunt at night. Big cats are so well camouflaged that they are hard to see. Stripes and spots blend in so well that we could walk right by a sleeping bobcat and never know it."

"We need to be very quiet in the meadow if we're going to see the animals," Patti said as they started off.

Just then Bobby shouted, "Look!" They all turned quickly, but most of them just saw rustling leaves as two deer darted away into a thicket.

"Oops, I forgot to be quiet. Sorry," said Bobby.

"That's OK," whispered Annie, "but be quiet now and turn around very slowly." This time Bobby was very quiet. They all turned slowly and saw a raccoon digging in the mud at the water's edge.

"What's he digging for?" whispered Annie.

"He's looking for food," Patti said softly. "Raccoons eat all sorts of things. Here they find snails and crayfish. See how raccoons seem to wash their food before they eat it? Over there is another raccoon catching fish!"

"Sometimes we can tell an animal is here without actually seeing it," said Patti. "This winding ridge in the dirt tells us that a mole has been burrowing here. Moles almost never come out of their burrows. They catch worms and bugs near the surface and live in deeper burrows that they line with soft grass and leaves."

All of a sudden, Molly gasped. "I see an armadillo!" she whispered loudly.

"We're lucky to see an armadillo so early in the day," said Patti. "Animals do different things at different times of the day just like you do. Armadillos usually come out to look for food later in the evening."

"Look at that bird," Ryan called. "I think it's hurt."

Patti chuckled, "That's what it wants you to think. That's a killdeer. It acts as if its wing were broken so that it can lead any dangerous intruders like us away from its nest. Let's go."

As they watched, a wild pig came loping out of the oak trees and headed toward the killdeer which flew off.

"Was it going to eat that bird?" Anita asked.

"No," Patti answered, "but wild pigs like to eat eggs. A wild pig will eat almost anything, even leftovers around the picnic area."

Suddenly a loud squabbling came from the trees. "What's making all that noise?"
Cassie asked.

Patti gestured for them to be quiet and led them around a clump of scrub oak trees.
There they watched two turkeys fighting to see which one would get to live in the tree.
"Lots of animals compete like this over territory," said Patti.

It was getting late so they started back down the trail. Ryan stopped short as a snake came slithering out from under some leaves. "We've been walking around out here with snakes?" he shouted.

Patti smiled. "Most of the snakes here are harmless," she said. "This scarlet snake is one of our prettiest snakes."

"Are there a lot of snakes here?" asked Ryan.

"Yes," said Patti. "We have over thirty different kinds, and although most of them won't hurt you, copperheads and rattlesnakes are poisonous. So, as with any wild animal, you shouldn't try to touch snakes."

"Oh," exclaimed Ryan, "you don't have to worry about that!"

As they returned to the visitor center, they passed a big pink bird swinging its head from side to side. "What a funny beak!" said Jimmy. "It looks like a spoon."

"That's why it's called a spoonbill," Patti said. "It uses its bill to scoop up small animals and fish from the shallow water."

Back at the visitor center, Patti told the children about some of the 450 wildlife refuges around the country. "Each one protects animals and plants that need our help. The wildlife refuges belong to all of us, and each one shows us how wild animals can be free and protected at the same time."

"That was fun," Ryan told Mr. Wilson as they got on the bus. "I'm going to find out what kinds of animals live at the other refuges."

"That's a good idea," said Mr. Wilson.

"Goodbye, thank you Patti," the children called. As they waved goodbye from the bus, a family of foxes stopped playing just long enough to watch them ride away.